Reflections for the Soul

By

George Calleja

Extract of praise to George Calleja

Emmaus… in today's society

I certainly encourage anyone to read this book and to be hopeful of their own journey back to God. God bless you and thank you George.

BY: SUSAN FARRUGIA

Her Silence

This work is a well-written personal testimonial of a special relationship with the Mother of God.

BY: LAWRENCE JAKOWS

Spiritual Reflections

George Calleja's book, Spiritual Reflections, would be a great read fo r any Christian, be they young or old.

BY: BRITTANY LEWIS

Waking up the sleeping giant

I am giving this book a 4 star because I don't like to give 5 stars to re ligious books because many don't believe and have a hard time conn ecting with a book like this.

BY: P.S.WINN

Heal my wounds

Really a great book, enjoyed the insights about healing, suffering and hope.

BY: FATHER STEPHEN GEMME

Taste and see that the Lord is Good

It is a little book that is full of much wisdom.

BY: AMY

Yes... I will follow Him

What touched me the most is the story of the author's personal response of "Yes". His story proved that there is a God and He is always there for each and every one of us.

BY: IRENE KUEH

My little book of daily prayer

Find peace, love and inspiration in this great little book of heart touching prayers.

BY: P.S.WINN

The Beatitudes… The Blessings from the Sermon on the Mount

The book was helpful and positive. It is easy to read and understand. It makes you want to be a better person and be closer to Jesus. I definitely recommend that you read this book!

BY: ROBERT A. HUNT

This book is dedicated to all the missionaries.

CONTENTS

Introduction

Then my soul will rejoice in the Lord and delight in his Salvation. (Psalm 35:9)

Truly my soul finds rest in God; my Salvation comes from him. (Psalm 62:1)

Yes, my soul, find rest in God; my hope comes from him. (Psalm 62:5)

Return to your rest, my soul, for the Lord has been good to you. (Psalm 116:7)

My soul is weary with sorrow; strengthen me according to your word. (Psalm 119:28)

It is a real pleasure for me as a Christian Author to have written another Christian book *'Reflections for the Soul'*, gathering short reflections I have written which have been posted on various social media of mine. These 35 short reflections have been grouped into seven themes, namely; Children, The Cross, Jesus, Love, Mary, Neighbour and Peace.

The aim of this book is that through these seven themes, the reader reflects upon the thoughts based on my personal experiences as well as those society goes through, and let these writings penetrate into the soul. These seven themes are also presented through a short Bible quotation, to further help the reader in his reflection.

These reflections are also being presented in this book with the aim of being shared with families, in Christian groups, in schools and universities, with politicians, and with anyone of good faith and in search of the Lord. I hope that these short reflections bring hope, courage, spiritual growth, healing and above all, that through them the soul be able to glorify God.

Thank you for making time to read this book and I wish each reader the blessings of the Lord.

George Calleja (Christian Author)

Chapter 1 - Children

Let the little children come to me, and do not hinder them, for the kingdom of God belongs to such as these. (Mark 10:14)

Children are to know and experience Jesus

Knowing and experiencing Jesus in one's life is of utmost importance for a person. I have witnessed this in my own life, through many people of different ages and cultures I have met, and who are interested to know Christ in a personal way and to follow Him through their life. Jesus is the source of life, who comforts, heals and above all, who paved the way to Salvation through dying on the Cross and the resurrection.

This truth is to be known and experienced by all humanity, even children. Today's children are the future adults of tomorrow's humanity. Tomorrow's society is based on what children learn today. Teaching children to know Jesus and experience Him in a personal way, paves the way for a better society in the future.

Adults need to feel responsible for teaching children about Jesus and to help them experience Him in their life even from their young and tender age.

Just like a little child

A little child totally depends on his mother for all his needs, freely and without hesitation approaches her to be embraced, to be loved, to be cared for, to be fed. The child's faith is totally entrusted unto his mother, without any questions asked, knowing that she is there at all times, and will provide for all his needs, always.

The mother, from the child's point of view is everything to him, is the source of his life, is the protector of his life, is everything. Isn't the mother like a *'god'* for the child?

This same trust of the child towards his mother, is an example of who Jesus is for us. Jesus, the Son of God, who died on the Cross, is our Saviour. He loves us, He cares for us, He feeds us with His spiritual food. Do we have the same confidence in Jesus, when compared to a child's trust towards his mother? Are we excited to meet Jesus, to be with Him and listen to what He has to say to us? If only our trust and excitement towards Jesus were like that of a child's towards his mother! Then our life would be fulfilled with His love and daily grace.

Loving our children

Do you recall the episode from the Bible in Luke 18:15-16 where it is written that 'People were also bringing babies to Jesus for him to place his hands on them. When the disciples saw this, they rebuked them. But Jesus called the children to him and said, "Let the little children come to me, and do not hinder them, for the kingdom of God belongs to such as these.'

These two particular verses explicitly show how much Jesus loved children, as they too belong to the kingdom of God. For Jesus, children who clearly also includes babies, are precious, are special, and belong to the Father.

This image of Jesus calling the children to him, puts a lot of responsibility on parents, educators and any other person to teach and show the way for children to be with Jesus. A good upbringing of children and a commitment to always love them as Jesus loved them, is a priority and of utmost importance for everyone in contact with children.

Loving children will pave their way for the kingdom of God.

Babies in their mothers' womb want to live

A couple of days ago I was in a chapel, praying, meditating and experiencing the Love of God in a personal way. It was a moment of peace, of knowing that God treasures me immensely. I was reflecting about life, of how wonderful it is, even when we face difficult moments in our life. In those precise difficult moments of life, God intervenes through His grace, to present us with His peace, His love, His care, His comfort… so as to experience His love in a personal way.

During this time of meditating, I also remembered about babies in their mothers' womb. Would these mothers accept their baby in their womb and let them live, to experience life, to be loved and experience the wonderful life God prepared for them? Or would some mothers, for whatever reason, deny their babies this wonderful experience?

Babies in their mothers' womb would want to live. They are God's gift not only to their mother and father… but to all humanity. They are a gift that God presents to humanity. When we love our neighbour, we are loving Jesus. When a mother loves her baby in her womb and accepts the baby to be born, she is loving Jesus. On the Cross Jesus suffered also for those mothers who deny a life to their unborn child.

Jesus called the children to go to Him. Let us pray that all mothers find the courage and support needed to accept their babies in their womb and let them live and experience through God's grace this wonderful life.

Today's children are the future generation

What we sow in today's children, is what we reap in future generations. This is so true and is evidently witnessed in today's society. The kind of upbringing of today's children, is what will be the foundation of tomorrow's society.

Parents have a big responsibility to shoulder upon themselves for the upbringing of their children. Christians and other people of different faiths and beliefs also have to shoulder such responsibility by what they teach and practice. Governments and other people that influence a country, also have to shoulder their responsibility through the laws that are enacted and that have a direct or indirect impact on today's children.

The formation of today's children rests upon each one of us. Today's society is responsible for future generations. What we sow in today's children, is what we reap in future generations, as today's children arc the future generation.

Chapter 2 - The Cross

Whoever wants to be my disciple must deny themselves and take up their Cross and follow me. (Mark 8:34)

Carrying the burdens of life

Every person in the world goes through various difficult moments in life. These difficulties, or so called, burdens of life, can take the form of sickness, being unemployed, family arguments, the death of a family member... and many, many such other examples.

What I have observed through life is, that different people who could be experiencing the same burdens of life, such as a particular sickness, can react differently to such similar situations. I have observed persons who, when faced with sickness, react angrily against God, placing the blame of their suffering on God. Such people carry the burden of their sickness by becoming bitter towards God, losing their inner peace and often end up living in despair.

On the other hand, I have also observed other people who, when faced with the same kind of sickness are at peace with themselves. These people have accepted their sickness knowing that God is with them, comforting them, loving them and giving them the necessary grace to carry their burden. The secret of these people is that they trust in Jesus, in His love for them, and know that through the Cross,

He carries the burdens of their life... their sickness. What a difference in the way to face suffering!

What do you do, when you are faced with a burden in your life? Do you offer your burdens to Jesus on the Cross? Do you feel Him carrying your burden with you?

Give Him everything

Jesus. The Son of God. The Son who died on the Cross.

The Cross that embraced all the sins and sufferings of all time of mankind. Through Jesus' love all the sins and sufferings were embraced.

Jesus waits for me to go to the Cross and give Him my everything.

My problems, my sufferings, my tensions, my sins... are to be taken to the Cross.

Go to Jesus, to the Cross and give your everything, emptying yourself, to become nothing.

And in this nothingness, the Father, through the Holy Spirit, feeds you with His grace, His wisdom, to proclaim His love to others.

Hold on to Jesus

On many occasions in life people go through difficult moments. It could be a time of despair and of losing one's faith.

When faced with any sort of difficulty in life, the secret is to trust in Jesus, even in the darkness. Jesus, through the Cross already lived that difficult moment for us. He took that difficult moment of our lives and through the Cross, transformed it into Salvation. After dying on the Cross, through His resurrection, Salvation became possible and was offered to all mankind.

So, whenever we face difficult moments in life, we are to be encouraged. We are to trust in Him completely, and to continuously hold on to Jesus, for Salvation is only possible through Him.

Jesus and the Cross

Do you ever dedicate time to reflect upon the episode narrating when Jesus died on the Cross? Do you know that when Jesus died on the Cross, He nailed all our sins to the Cross and set us free?

Jesus died on the Cross because He loves you. He embraced the Cross out of love to set you free from all sins, to set you free from your lack of faith. He is Jesus, the Son of God.

When Jesus embraced the Cross, He was embracing you, embracing the same cross you carry in your daily life. The daily cross you carry in your life, is *'lighter'* to carry if you trust in Him.

We are to be another Jesus in our life, by being Jesus to others. Embracing our cross in our life, through the grace and love of Jesus, is one way of being Jesus to others.

Embracing our cross is embracing Jesus.

The Cross is love

Have you ever wondered about the Cross that Jesus died on? Do you really believe that Jesus died on the Cross for you? You might ask, but why did He die for me on the Cross?

The only reason Jesus died for you on the Cross is because He loves you. Yes, Jesus loves you. It is good to understand and believe that the Cross is the love of Jesus. His suffering, His death on the Cross was completed through His resurrection. His love for you through the Cross is His resurrection, the forgiveness of sin, so that you may be able to receive His grace, His peace and above all His Salvation.

So rejoice through His Cross for His love is always present.

Chapter 3 - Jesus

The next day John saw Jesus coming toward him and said, "Look, the Lamb of God, who takes away the sin of the world! (John 1:29)

Believe in Him

Believing in Him brings the fullness of life to all. Having faith and believing in Jesus, the Son of God, brings richness to life.

Many people doubt Jesus or do not believe at all in Him. There are many other people who do not doubt Jesus and totally believe in Him.

These people's view of life is somewhat different. The difference of how they view life can be seen when they are faced by illness, the death of a relative, family problems, broken relationships, and so much more.

Believing in Him and having faith in Jesus helps you to overcome these difficulties, to be able to live them through His love, and to always to love your neighbour.

Christ... is the way

Many roads lead to different places. Many adverts tell you what to buy and what your needs are. Many people say that they know it all!

But 'the way', the way to Salvation, the way that takes us to God the Father, is Jesus Christ.

Christ is the way, He is the only one that can take us there.

Follow Him... Get to know Him in a personal way, and let Him show you the WAY.

Jesus is everything

When I reflect about my life, upon the years that passed by, I come to a conclusion that Jesus is everything in my life. The mercy and forgiveness I received from Him, His constant love for me, His daily grace and care to me, made me truly believe that He loves me dearly.

Now I understand the reason why He died on the Cross. He died for me, for you, to have this relationship with Him.

My prayer is that we grow to know Jesus more in our lives, and to follow Him everywhere.

You are everything for Jesus. Is He everything for you?

Lord Jesus

Lord Jesus,

my prayer before I sleep tonight,

is that people all over the world get to know your love for them.

I pray for those people who have rejected you,

Lord give them the opportunity to know you.

Lord I pray for those who persecute you,

that they may find you.

I pray for the children who are dying in wars,

that you may bless their soul.

Lord may your peace reign,

may the leaders of the countries understand your Love,

and instead of resorting to wars,

declare peace throughout the world.

Thank you Jesus,

Amen.

You… Jesus

You.

Jesus.

The Saviour of my life.

The One whom I entrust my life to.

The giver of my life.

You.

Jesus.

The Healer of my life.

The One who loves me dearly.

The helper of my life.

Oh Jesus.

I thank you for everything.

For you show me the way,

how to love my neighbour.

To help them, to feed them, to listen to them,

To bring them to You.

You.

Jesus.

You are my everything.

You are the source of life,

and I will do your will.

Chapter 4 - Love

Love is patient, love is kind. It does not envy, it does not boast, it is not proud. (1 Corinthians 13:4)

God's love is ever lasting

God's love for all mankind is ever lasting. God, the creator of male and female, loves all mankind in such a deep way, in such a personal way, that it is ever lasting. The depth of His love for each and every person is so enormous, that no words exist to explain this ever lasting love, that has no beginning and no end.

Mankind has the opportunity to accept God's love and receive it freely by loving one's neighbour. Our neighbour, being a creation of God is a very treasured and precious person for God. The way and the depth of our love for our neighbour, reflects how much we truly love God.

If God's love is ever lasting, we ought to love our neighbour in the best possible way, that is to love unconditionally.

I am to love every person

I am to love every person. This is what Jesus asks of me. This is what Jesus did and preached.

To every person I am to offer His love. Who is this person who I am to love?

My neighbour, whom I meet during every moment of my life.

My neighbour is the person whom I am to love.

Jesus loves this person.

Life... is all about loving

Many times we hear of stories about life. We hear and read stories about the life of famous people. We know about the life of our close relatives, of our own family members. We know the story of our own life.

In any person's life there would be the good and happy moments, or the bad and sad moments. Each of these moments would have their own particular story, a particular situation to recall. Each moment in life, each situation we encounter in life, is a particular moment that requires love. Life... is all about loving.

As human beings we are all called to love. We are all called to love our neighbour. Each human being, coming from whichever country in the world, practicing whichever religion, has a golden rule to follow... to love.

As a Christian, practicing the golden rule of love means to be another Jesus to my neighbour. In every moment of my life, in any situation I find myself in, love is to be the characteristic of my life… that is Jesus. Being Jesus is to share the love of the Father to all the people I encounter in every situation of my life.

So, if life is all about loving, why is peace lacking in life? Because love is not being practised and shared by all. Love requires to be reciprocal. Peace is the answer to reciprocal love, while disunity is the result of lack of love.

This is what I really would like all to understand, that life is all about loving. Whatever your life is about, whatever situation you find yourself in… you can always choose to love. Love is the answer to your life.

Love… brings peace to life

Many people talk about the importance of having peace in life. Peace is not just about not having wars… of not arguing in families. Peace is the result of love between nations… between people.

Love… brings peace to life. Love is what Jesus practiced, preached, lived. The love that Jesus gave us, is the love we are to give to others.

Do you want to bring peace to life? Do you want to see the world living in peace?

Give the love of Jesus to others, and where this love is lived, there will be peace in life.

Radiate God's love to others

Being a Christian is to radiate God's love to others. Radiating God's love is possible whenever you are one with your neighbour.

Wherever there is suffering, be Jesus to others. Wherever there is an argument, bring peace amongst all. When you meet a person who has lost hope in life, show him Jesus, who will embrace him in a personal way.

Every Christian can radiate the love of God to others. Whenever this is done, joy, peace and hope is present.

Chapter 5 - Mary

"I am the Lord's servant," Mary answered. "May your word to me be fulfilled." Then the angel left her. (Luke 1:38)

Life is for everyone

Every morning and in every moment of my life, I thank God for my existence. I thank my parents for educating me and being with me in every moment of my life.

Life is a joy to live, even when one faces difficult moments. The joy of life only comes through God, the God who created us, and loves each person in a personal way.

Life is for everyone. The joy of life was already present in the womb of Mary. For in Luke 1:44, we find that Elizabeth, upon hearing Mary's greeting when visiting her, proclaimed that, 'the baby in my womb leaped for joy....''

Let the babies in their mothers' womb live, let them experience the joy of life.

Every person in the world is called to love, to love all mankind and to love the babies in their mothers' womb. Life is for everyone... including all unborn babies.

Mary is an example for welcoming a child

You have surely heard the story of Mary being the mother of Jesus. You surely know about the 'yes' that Mary said to the angel upon announcing to her that she would become the mother of God. The 'yes' of Mary meant that she was ready to serve and fulfil the mission entrusted to her by God.

Mary went through a lot of hardship and suffering but also of joy being the mother of Jesus. This was possible as Mary always lived by that 'yes' to God's will.Mary, is a true example to today's society and brings encouragement to all woman carrying a child in their womb. The great example of Mary is to be lived and imitated by all woman carrying a child in their womb, that is to say the 'yes'… 'yes, I will give birth to my child, in suffering and in joy, to be beside my child while growing up and give the best love to my child'.

Mary is an example for welcoming a child.

Mary is an example of how to love

Mary, the Mother of Jesus is not mentioned much in the Bible. From the little episodes starting by The Annunciation (Luke 1:26-38) and followed by The Visitation (Luke 1:39-45), The Magnificat (Luke 1:46-56), and when the angel appeared to Joseph in a dream (Matthew 1:18-21), The Nativity (Luke 2:1-7) and the visit of the Magi (Matthew 2:9-12), followed by the episode of Simeon at the presentation of the Christ-child (Luke 2:28-35) and the adventure of the flight to Egypt (Matthew 2:13-15), followed by the finding of the Christ Jesus in the Temple (Luke 2:40-52) and reading about the Son of Mary (Mark 6:3), followed by Mary at the wedding feast at Cana (John 2:1-11) and later with John at the Cross (John 19:26-27), up until the final episode of Mary at the upper room during Pentecost (Acts of the Apostles 1:12-14), we find one common virtue of Mary throughout these episodes. This is the virtue of love.

Mary loved unconditionally in all the episodes mentioned in the Bible, and for sure also in other situations she found herself in, which are not known about.

It is good to go through these episodes, to read them as narrated in the Bible and to meditate about them.

For sure there is a lot what one can learn from Mary, which is the art of loving. Mary, the Mother of Jesus loved the Father tremendously, and her 'yes' at the Annunciation paved the way through the Trinity, to be the Mother of us all.

Get to know more about Mary, and I am sure your life would be blessed, and you will be strengthened to love as Mary loved.

The Queen of the Universe

Mary, the Mother of Jesus.

The Mother of all families.

The Mother of all nations.

The Mother of all generations.

Mary, who walks with us to Jesus.

To know Him.

To embrace Him.

To follow Him.

Mary, full of love.

Full of obedience.

Full of comfort.

Full of holiness.

Mary, the Immaculate Conception.

The Mother of God.

The Voice of the suffering.

The Queen of the Universe.

We are to live like Mary

Mary, the mother of Jesus, wept upon seeing her Son dying on the Cross. Mary, embraced that particular moment of suffering, of seeing Her Son covered in blood, dead, but knowing that the Cross would bring the Salvation to all humanity.

In her suffering, Mary, as a mother accepted the will of the Father, that of being the Mother of Jesus. In her silence, she suffered, but that suffering was 'nothing', knowing that Salvation was only possible through the Cross… the Cross that reaped the joy of Salvation.

Today, Mary is still with us. We are to imitate Mary in our lives, to bring that source of love, comfort and forgiveness which Mary presented to the world in a humble way, and to give it to society.

We are to present Mary, through our life, in our families, at school, at university, at our workplace, in parliament, and wherever we are and with whomever we are with. Mary is to be present in our society, by presenting Jesus as the Saviour of humanity.

As much as we are to know Jesus in a personal way, so to show us the way to Salvation, we are also to know Mary in our lives. Discovering Mary, is discovering the treasure of love. Her love was of doing the will of the Father, not only of being the Mother of Jesus… but of being the Mother of all humanity.

Today, Mary, wants us to return to Jesus. Today, Mary, is praying for humanity… for our society. Today, we are to live like Mary.

Chapter 6 - Neighbour

"A new command I give you: Love one another. As I have loved you, so you must love one another. By this everyone will know that you are my disciples, if you love one another." (John 13:34-35)

Help the person next to you

Every moment in our lives we have an opportunity to love. Every person who is next to us is our neighbour. We are to help, to love, to comfort our neighbour.

Our neighbour is precious, because Jesus died for each and everyone of us… including our neighbour.

Help the person next to you, help your neighbour, for Salvation is for all.

Life is beautiful

Life is beautiful.

For in life there is you, my neighbour.

My neighbour, who is happy, who is sad.

My neighbour, who is healthy, who is weak.

My neighbour, who is rich, who is poor.

How beautiful life is.

When I am with my neighbour,

to cherish the moments of happiness,

to comfort the moments of sadness.

My neighbour makes my life fulfilled.

For when I am with my neighbour,

there in the midst is Jesus.

Life with Jesus is beautiful.

Serving others

Serving others is a way to bring Jesus to the people. Serving through His Love is a way to evangelise. Many people are in need of help. Many people are waiting for His Love.

We are to serve others, to serve our neighbour. We are to say 'yes', just as Mary did... and serve, serve, serve.

Through serving others, we will be fulfilled. We will be in peace through His grace. Serving our neighbour gives them an opportunity to experience love, to meet Jesus.

Tomorrow... a day to love my neighbour

Tomorrow is another day in our lives. We go to work, to school, clean the house, play some sports, visit the doctor.

Tomorrow, is another challenge in our lives. The challenge to love my neighbour.

Tomorrow… I will love my workmates, obey and respect my teacher, put the house in order to love my family… tomorrow is another opportunity to love every person I am with moment by moment.

I hope that tomorrow turns out that I have loved every person I meet.

Tomorrow, will you love your neighbour?

Your neighbour is Jesus

Who is your neighbour in the present moment? Do you know your neighbour? How do you get along with your neighbour?

Neighbours are found everywhere. They could be your next door neighbour, your school mate, your work colleague, your parish priest, your doctor… with whoever you meet in your daily life, that is your neighbour.

Have you ever realized that your neighbour is Jesus? Maybe it is difficult to understand it… but yes, in your neighbour there is Jesus. What a great opportunity it is, that whenever you meet your neighbour… you love him, as you be loving Jesus.

Are you loving your neighbour? Are you loving Jesus? Remember, your neighbour is Jesus.

Chapter 7 - Peace

"Blessed is the king who comes in the name of the Lord!" "Peace in heaven and glory in the highest!" (Luke 19:38)

Being in peace

Being in peace with one another is something that many people wish to experience. Peace is possible when we love our neighbour, when we help our neighbour, when we forgive our neighbour.

Everybody is to try and live for peace, that is to bring peace wherever one might be.

Peace is only possible when we love one another and to let Him be the center of our lives.

Jesus is the source to bring peace to all. Are we letting Jesus to bring this peace?

Being in peace with my neighbour

Being in peace with my neighbour… oh, how wonderful it is.

Being in peace with my neighbour, is an opportunity to increase the love in the world. If all the people had to really live in peace with their neighbour, the world would be different.

Let us change the world, let us bring peace in the world… by first being in peace with my neighbour.

How to bring peace to the world

The world is crying for peace. Many people ask, but how is it possible, to have peace in the world? At times we think that this is not possible. The many episodes that we witness nowadays really make us wonder if peace is possible.

But peace is possible. It all depends upon each person. The only responsibility that each person has is, to love one's neighbour. Imagine if every person were to take up this challenge and loved his neighbour. Peace would be possible.

Peace in the world only depends on loving our neighbour. Loving your neighbour is possible by loving Jesus.

Peace be with you

Peace to all in the world, I want to give this peace to all... which is the peace of Jesus.

Share this peace of Jesus, pray for one another and trust always in Him.

At least during this day, say 'Peace be with you!' to your neighbour, and live in peace with one another.

The peace of Jesus is for all.

Today... let us live for peace

Today, at this early morning, as I woke up, I said thank you Jesus for this lovely day.

I told Jesus that today I would live to bring peace in every situation of my life, with every person I meet.

I really wish and pray that you join me in this prayer, to live for peace in the world.

For sure, the day would turn out to be lovelier if I succeeded in really living for peace during the day.

Wishing you all have a peaceful day and that by God's grace, you love your neighbour.

About the Author

George Calleja grew up in Malta and is married with two children. In 2009 he obtained his MBA through the University of Leicester.

During the years 1990 to 1996 he was a full-time missionary with 'The International Catholic Programme for Evangelisation - ICPE' and evangelised in various countries such as Russia, Ghana, Poland, Germany, and Malta amongst others. Since 1997, he has been an active member of the Focolare Movement in Malta.

In 2012 George embarked on a mission of evangelisation through the use of various social media. His first Christian book 'Peace and Unity in our lives – Volume One' was published in November 2014. Since then, he has published another 15 Christian books focusing on various themes. His writings are also published in various other Christian social media, such as *Laikos* and *Catholic365.com*.

Being a dedicated Christian writer, George Calleja is actively involved in spreading the Good News through various means on social media. His writings on blogs and various prominent websites, together with his podcasts and videos, make him an example of how to evangelise in today's society through technology.

His latest evangelisation project is that of providing online Christian courses, namely 'Living the Beatitudes in your life', 'How to heal your spiritual wounds' and *'Getting to know about Mary's silence'*, all available through Udemy. Furthermore, George Calleja evangelises through his YouTube Channel with his Christian programme *'God Loves You', 'How to live your life for Christ'* and the *'30 Second Clip'*.

Connect with the Author

If you would like to contact the author, please email him at: *peacethroughunity@gmail.com*

You can also follow him through the following social links:-

Blog:

http://peacethroughunity.blogspot.com/

FaceBook:

https://www.facebook.com/georgecallejaebooks/timeline

GoodReads:

https://www.goodreads.com/author/show/9847194.George_Calleja

Instagram:

https://www.instagram.com/george_calleja_author/

Smashwords:

https://www.smashwords.com/profile/view/geocalpeace

Spotify:

https://open.spotify.com/show/6xDW2IaQcnWtRBAmpjT39D

Twitter:

https://twitter.com/PeaceUnityLives

Udemy:

https://www.udemy.com/user/george-calleja/

Website:

https://sites.google.com/site/peaceinunity/

WordPress:

http://peacethroughunity.wordpress.com/

YouTube Channel:

https://www.youtube.com/channel/UCkS4BJLIeodVZAS8i6Sn6Og

Future books to be published

Writing Christian books is a passion in the life of the author. His passion is that of seeking to bring peace to the world, to make it a better place to live in and to draw people closer to God. As a Catholic, it has become his mission to share the love of God through his writings. The joy of sharing the love of God with the reader is tremendous and it uplifts his life and also that of his family.

For these reasons, the author is always planning ahead about what to write next. In 2023, George Calleja will be publishing another Christian book focusing on the unborn child, which you are encouraged to look out for.

For further information about his publications, please visit his FaceBook page at:

https://www.facebook.com/georgecallejaebooks/timeline

or visit the authors official website 'George Calleja – Christian Author' at:

https://sites.google.com/site/georgecallejachristianauthor/

Published books

'The King of the peripheries' – November 2021

'Emmaus… in today's society' – November 2020

'Come to Me' – September 2019

'Her Silence' – January 2019

'In His image' – June 2018

'Spiritual Reflections' – December 2017

'Waking up the sleeping giant' – July 2017

'Heal my Wounds' - February 2017

'The Light' - September 2016

'Taste and see that the Lord is good' - April 2016

'My Little Book of Daily Prayer' - January 2016

'The Beatitudes… the blessings from the Sermon on the Mount' - September 2015

'Evangelization through Social Networking Sites' - June 2015

'Peace and unity in our lives' - March 2015

'Yes… I Will Follow Him' - March 2015

'Peace and unity in our lives - Volume Two' - January 2015

'Peace and unity in our lives - Volume One' - November 2014

While thanking you for reading 'Reflections for the Soul', I hope that it has helped you to increase your faith and to draw you closer to God. As an independent author, the success of my books relies mostly on reviews and recommendations by readers such as yourself. If you have found this book useful, please tell others about it… your family, your friends and others. I highly appreciate your assistance to share about this book and to share about God's love.

Thank you and God bless you!
George Calleja (Christian Author)

www.ingramcontent.com/pod-product-compliance
Lightning Source LLC
Chambersburg PA
CBHW060952130726
48001CB00014B/1083